Certain Roses

Angela Livingstone

Certain Roses

Poems 1980 - 2010

Certain Roses: Poems 1980 - 2010
published in the United Kingdom in 2017
by Leslie Bell trading as Mica Press
47 Belle Vue Road, Wivenhoe, Colchester, Essex CO7 9LD

www.micapress.co.uk | books@micapress.co.uk

ISBN 978-1-869848-15-6

Acknowledgement:
versions of 'Snowstorm' and 'Winter Morning' were first published in *Modern Poetry in Translation*.

Contents

Winter solstice....1
The path 2
Lerryn woods 3
Certain roses 4
Dragonfly 5
Dog-rose season 6
Woodlands resurgent 7
The vine....8
Metka 9
At a conference in Moscow 10
The perfect taxi-driver 11
To T. Doherty 12
Death 14
Cremation 15
Death of Brodsky....17
On living when others have died 18
Passing the scrap-iron yard....20
The grabs next day 21
Airport 22
For Oliver Bernard....24
The nearest I can get 25

The bells of St Mary's Church at East Bergholt 26
Words 27
The word 'transference' 28
A cry / *A chime* 30
Love 31
After Pasternak...32
Location 33
To Geoffrey Hill 34
She 36
Leaving 37
Friendship in autumn...38
'Snowstorm' 40
'Winter morning' 42
Thistle...44
Notes..45

Winter solstice

Knuckle-bone sun,
how you've punched yourself in,
rehearsing old battles,
and stuck like a clenched fist
in cloud-white cladding.

If our prayers can prise you
free into capable
life, lift us
from cliff-edges, crevices,
strict cracks in dead brick,

and spread, sun, sky -
wide your fine fingers,
fling through our windows
your palmfuls, armfuls,
of brightness and daring -

The path

If you turn a corner
into the high-walled
footpath narrowly
winding in shadow
uphill from the road –

all of a sudden
the enclosing groan
and drum and roar
of traffic vanish.
All of a sudden –

a footstep silence:
lumps felt
under mud by feet.
The path's walls -
wide as moors.

Lerryn woods

(thinking of Wallace Stevens while walking in steep woodlands)

to look at these
leaves and not
name them beech
or leaves even
nor time them autumn

to step on stiff
moss or shifting
stone and not
house them in
honed symbols

to grip and climb
a hundred kinds
of old hard-grown
gapped and twining
pleached-root footholds

and not think of
sense or purpose
only know
the nothing that is
there, the wordless

Certain roses

Those rounded tiny roses
patched and deformed by weather
who've lived too long in the dying
traffic-dust front-gardens –

how can they be so red?
The broken red, known to me,
red, streaked and cracking –
it's nothing if not definite.

I'll translate them: stop
torpor and trance, be quick
to steal a bunch of stalks,
of bunched instructive thorns.

Now I am taking palmfuls
of the severe dark petals,
and dropping them in my pocket:
transient, talismanic.

Dragonfly

He came as Inspector of Ponds,
He'd got the uniform on –
Royal blue and peacock-green.
He was straight as an aeroplane,
Abrupt as a switch of plan,
More radiant than kings and queens.

Staring, he hung in the sun,
Then, sharp as a knife-blade, span
(By some map of infallible signs)
Like a wind to the opposite end,
Measured the charms of the pond,
Shone like a jewel, and was gone.

Dog-rose season

this is the dog-rose season and the cistus,
the tender season which precedes the glorious,
when foxgloves lean on the breeze, with never-famous
cow-parsley and thistle; while straying goose-grass –
suddenly weft with tiny star-like stitches –
catches stems and tendrils, clambers, clutches,
trammels nettle, alkanet and lychnis.

Woodlands resurgent

A million million never-repeated shapes,
or if repeated never known to be,
oblivious of their own oblivion,
flare up and spread like buds and stalks of fire,
thrusting down into thickets, streaming across
fences to fathom every emptiness -

Not only shapes but systems, laws and ways
are there, all kinds of silent categories,
substance and nuance, fragrance, subtleties
we'll never ponder, grand perfected growths
and untold potencies already banked
there, luminous like centuries of wealth.

What is all this, the green and green and green,
yet none of it green's final modelling?
What is this mass of treasure never spent:
spikes, tendrils, foliage, branches trammelling sky,
what store of the untellable? Like far
stars, yet dense as earth, surrounding us.

The vine

I pulled the limbs of the vine across the shed-roof
trying to preserve them, give them room under the sun.
They were heavy, unwilling to move, and fragile,
they seemed to want to lie in a heap in some corner
like big old spiders surrounded by webby breakage.
I set up hooks and stiff green strings, and dragged them
into the place I'd determined, though I felt sorry –
– better perhaps to have chopped them off at the trellis,
thrown those wild things away, for the sake of neatness.
Why am I saving great growths of snapping greenery
with a few hard grapes among them in bloodless bunches?
All this is so – delicate, so exhausting.

Metka

Metka, you've come from your vegetable plot
with a basket of beet and a handful of marigold,
your hands have cleft stiff earth, your feet
are in mud-path boots, your heart – full of music.
Are you clearing out griefs from the ground like weeds?
Are you starting the wintry planting of *metta*?

At a conference in Moscow

for Mikhail Gasparov

Swift as a dark-plumed bird, the philosopher
flew unsuspected down to me and bowed,
spreading wide wings or floating cloak, and tore
the slant black hat from his surprising brow
to touch the floor. I, suddenly a queen,
estranged, enchanted by his gesture, stared
at the grand, thoughtful, gaunt, intrepid man.
Years later: haunted by his flight, his grace.

The perfect taxi-driver

switched off the radio –

wore London like a glove –

slid along side-roads –

arrived at the station

with two brave minutes

to spare / I flew

down sparse exhilarant

crowds to the brink:

the train – a gondola.

To T. Doherty

Your being here, Terence, your passionate talking and caring,
your sharing yourself,
your full heart and full head
which you kept giving out to us all, like everyone's birthday,
your bursting-out laughter –

your sudden reciting of poetry
once, to a sad little boy you had met,
enchanting him into a carefree dream
while you whirled your life past him
(as if you were tossing him wonderful sea-sides and gardens) –
your garden, your purple and dark-red and silver
plants, which you alone knew all the names of
and told us so cheerfully: tree-peony, hellebore . . .
buoyant names! And the wisdom, the speech
of your sculptures and pictures!
– whatever odd portion of space or of silence
you chanced on, you just didn't rest till you'd steeped it
in vigorous beauty . . .

To put it quite simply: you made the world better,
and people: the dull became brighter, the solemn
started to smile; and – again and again –
those who were locked in an ancient decorum
were freed by your jokes, your rebellion.

* * *

You got us all listening, paying attention.
Only, it wasn't so much to yourself
as to all you revealed: to the world
of history, the evolution of species,
miraculous flora and fauna, art
and architecture. Other men's genius.

We felt we could listen for ever.
We must have forgotten to tell you
the world would be dreadfully altered
without you in it. . . Alas,
we just weren't good enough listeners.
We didn't attend to your sadness.

Death

She feels it ripening
within her and growing
like an unplanned being.

When this being is born
earth and sky will crackle
as when flames catch fences,

or seed-pods, dehiscent,
crack, and their heart scatters:
pale wings in a rainfall.

Cremation

for Valya Coe

I was cradling
pink roses and
pink-tipped white ones,

their stems in my
hand, heads on my
arm - cherishing,

protecting them
all the way down
from Essex by

early trains and
rainy roadways
of dark London,

defending them
fearfully from
danger, steering

trustful exposed
petals through rough
crowds – until I

laid them, alas,
in lethally
savage flames, then

travelled back home
with empty hand,
with bereft arm.

Death of Brodsky

Brodsky is dead. A big left molar is aching.
The snow 'that cureth all' has disappeared.
Sunshine – a silver knife in a clutter of bracken.

I catch quite unpredicted a sob in the open
Essex lane and my eye undertakes the weight
of a tear. Is this from toothache? Or the waking

thought that the poet has, doubly now, abandoned
the moody Baltic marshland where nothing stopped
his gaze, and the lovely cruel canals that flooded

palaces and all Russia, untransferable,
whose fate I'm gathering conscientiously
from poets, syllable by syllable.

On living when others have died

We're living in the after-life of lives.
Our minutes are those minutes and those hours
some confidently called their future, then
failed to inhabit, leaving them as ours.

Even one who pressed to the very edge
of Now – like someone staring in, face smack
against the window, vivid with argument
and indignation – failed and faltered back.

Our filled-up bodies, our all-filling talk,
politics, prayers, our weathers blue or grey,
our science and love and music - all are nought,
mere blank space with every star blacked out,

from their (gone) point of view, to their (decayed)
discernment. Not one object where I am
exists for them. So, have they been betrayed?
Him so admired, her so much called upon,

I derelicted – dropped into "the past" –
that instant he, she, froze all his, all her
warm being into so-called "memory".
I gave up hope of seeing them, and preferred

that this additional, broken-off for each
of them, this never-more-continuing time,
continue airy to my avid breath.
They're paralysed. We walk along the beach,

and take our children to the pantomime.

Passing the scrap-iron yard

A marked leap of the heart –
not at a skylark,
not for the celandine,
rainbows nor shafts of rain,

but this madly swaying crab,
this drunken star,
bent teeth snatching at scrap:
the black mechanical grab.

Steel magnolia-flower,
high snare of curved
fingers, power-
fully plunging, it swerves,

lurches from vast
heights to smashed heaps,
takes, ravishes
things made of iron and rust.

The grabs next day

Thunder was thundering. I thought: “In this downpour
the grabs won’t be working, the men will be in.”
I got there (my ankles and shoulders all flowing)
and the men were in oilskins, the grabs were thundering,
staggering, shouting in teemings of rain.
Then I thought: “Thank the Lord, the whole earth is alive,
the sky in a passion, and these ancient machines,
drunken, clanking, are one with the storm.”

Airport

After the shops and the slogans,
past Costa's superior café,
after the passport-controlling
and the lights of the duty-free section,
heading for gate number eighty –
unforeseen, an enchantment.

Sudden, below, in a hollow,
with a staircase winding round it,
two-man-tall and leaning,
spreading silver, flowing
with frail and infinite fringes –
a cone of resplendent metal.

A pyramid, a chiseling
of ripples (just where I'd got to
pass, according to schedule),
and down its serenely swerving
mind-widening surface
white water-lace falling.

Of course it recalled the broken
waves on some moonlit shore-line,
but a shore that's all rolled and narrowed
into the form of a funnel,

or a skirt of embroidery edgings
with the white silk shining through them.

I glanced up – there was the artist's
face in a photo, smiling,
so imperturbably pleasant
I thought: anywhere but an airport
I'd never have loved this object,
this commissioned water-sculpture.

Still, as I wandered onward,
fearful, heaving my rucksack
towards the eightieth exit,
something in me was delighted.

For Oliver Bernard

Endless sky and endless land,
Trees trees trees, the mauve
Gold undergrowth of June,
Somewhere a samovar and stove,
Fabled sills carved out in wood.

Every village halts the train.
Petersburg is journeying
South in never-stopping talk.
Furious with everything
Our conductress elbows through.

I could write – I read instead:
"Moon and harbour, Walberswick",
Summon that shore, that estuary,
Put them down in Russia thick
With silver birch in the white night.

The nearest I can get

I long for long lines and third persons and absence of rhyme
and wildly evocative adjectives conjuring place
such as prairie or steppeland with outlines of riders far off
on misty horizons . . . But none of it comes:
instead the old brevity,
breathless and lyric,
and I,
panegyric,
enchanted by gravity,
staring at sky.

The bells of St Mary's Church at East Bergholt

Their timeless plunge into time –
their yield to ecstasy –
was like a swimmer reeling
off warm planks of a pier
into freezing waters.

They fell like man-overboard,
struck hard against the current
with terrible cries from below,
swung out like the soul of a drowner
in the iron-fast hold of a rescuer.

And hove like dolphins, surged
like whales through a keening sea,
devoured whole mountains of silence,
gouging out gorges of sounding,
sparing no one and nothing,

breaking our ears with their music.

For these five bells, good church,
I'm thankful, and for all
souls that have shouted or sung
or signalled aloud to me,
and all savage voices of truth.

Words

"Earth" gravely starts with "er-", or primal "ur-",
the grunt and stutter of antiquity,
then runs aground in mossy lisp of "th-th-":
so much a truer name than disyllabic
'térra', 'zemliὰ' or '`Erde'? Look, and we

found a fine syllable for sky: "sky" sleeps
inside our mouth: "ss-kk-", then wakes, takes flight
on soaring double vowel, unstoppable,
sustaining birds and climbs of cloud, the realms
of spirit, all the timeless tracks of night.

Biblical voices praised the name of the Lord
yet called him "nameless", praised the unnameable name.
But we can praise these all-pronouncing names:
they share the arcane shapes of sky and earth
and help us mention mysteries, walk through flame.

The word 'transference'

We used to press the watered secret stamps
onto the backs of our hands, and what delight
we felt to see the picture sliding out,
sometimes in fragile jigsaw-images
rainily breaking away at the floating edges
and sometimes – miracle! – an entire world
lightly transferred and transient on our skin.

This tender word, this lucid 'transference',
is cousin to such different ferrying:
'transport' – to London or to ecstasy,
'translation' – lifting out from speech to speech,
and 'metaphor' – a carefully fathomed shift
of meaning across meaning, or one vision
unfolded in the fabric of another.

While in the psychic underworld this name
darkens with mists, unseen ravines, who knows
what awful gorges, none of it comes clear
on held-out hands but, lost, I have to hook
my broken rope up onto shadowy ledges –
if only it will grip and lift me out
and over, to survival! Then – transfer

to somewhere else, with trellises and trees:
to pure pragmatic gardening – dig a pond,
get frogs to hop and irises to sway,
lean on a rake in the rain till all the sky
is printed like a transfer on my face,
entire! it floats and changes when I smile
and, if you look across, transfers to you.

A cry / *A chime*

someone was strangely

down from streaming

shouting *cloudy*

mountains **screaming**

surely endangering

sanity *loudly*

curtains of rain fell

sheltering the **"Save me!"**

pounded fading

sound of a lone bell

Love

the delicate boundary Akhmatova found

between people in love or **the naming of love**

shall build up instantly barbarous barricades

not in love which she managed respectful

of high barbed wire and mountainous rocks

with rifles ranged at the top *to cherish*

ah so much fineness **alas such violence**

how those gloved hands would quiver **I only**

shouted one syllable – down crashed the schlagbaum

crawl away painfully *patient eternally*

After Pasternak

On my arrival, there was long applause.
Now the bare stage, like a town square at dawn.
All round it the infinity of watchers,
rings of binoculars all trained on me.

I lean against a door for my turn to speak.
Then "Look," I'll say, "the reason I spurn this role..."
(God but you know it, though it's you who offer
the cup of blood, the hot distracting cup

I never dreamt of, striding towards the theatre)
"the reason's what you know: *another* play
is being performed, this drama of the cup
is only one of two. Please let me go…"

And yet my fingers curve to the fine stem,
my lips are already pursed for the sharp drops.
I'll act it out. Perhaps they'll cheer at the end.
But will my other role be kept for me?

Location

I, though, am not exactly here.
I'm making my way through another space.
(They may not have noticed this about me).
Hardly able to say: where.

Miles of feathergrass never seen,
famines (I never heard the keening),
deferences, endurances,
hardly to be imagined,

disappearances down bare roads.
And log-houses forever grow
back into forest, their earthen stoves
so large that men may bathe in them,

using the heat. Worship heat
for the cold will rip the skin from your tongue
with some of its flesh, if you idiotically
lick a spade. Wise fish

are fished through ice. During dancing,
drunken feet cleave to earth –
beyond me, steep as a scarp within me.
I cling and slide – it's a kind of climbing.

To Geoffrey Hill

Your girl of long ago, not
quite desired though quite regretted,
has died at sixty-three, you say
in your alarm of time. I'm
older, not in the rage you're in.

Perhaps we overlap in loss
at Rilke's elegies, for where I am,
no less, "is not Duino":
that biting storm, that voice of triumphant pain,
toothed and winged me too.

Rilke's abandonment of crying
loudly to angels in a louder wind;
then his perceiving (1912 postmodern?)
the whole world as 'interpreted' –
walking along the cliff-top back to the castle,

grasping that there's nothing more to do
but say so, blindingly,
and afterwards turn,
torn,
down, like the warm Egyptian,

down to the pots, the pen, and the thrown
word (as 'fountain', 'tower', or possibly 'chimney');
his giddy letting go of gentian height
and rounding up of firmer, lowland things
which crave performance –

these deeds were veins of silver in the earth
of youth for me
or, putting it more lastingly, a thin
fire inside the solidity of time,
breathing in time.

She

She grew too old, too bold, became enchanted.
Sallow cheeks belied an eldritch heat.
Neck as creased as nightmare-ridden sheets.
But the sword in the blood was deathless, her heart chanted.
With never a clever speech "in praise of age",
she stepped, quite secret, one foot crooked, down
the yellowing fields in small autumnal rain.
Flaming, exultant, spellbound, crazed, enraged.

Leaving

No, in a place of high reputations and rivalry
I cannot breathe - even at its most pure-hearted;
some may inhabit mildly those furious regions
but air for me is at lonelier stonier levels.
I won't join any throng,
nor drink wine in any fine congregation of scholars.
Thanks, but I'm leaving now, with sycamore leaves in my pockets,
stepping on palpable cobbles, not looking back.

Friendship in autumn

for Alan

The orchard's ragged floor is gold with moss.
Like yellow handkerchiefs, a few leaves float
on stringy twigs, we laugh through fallen fruit
and find a single bristling tree of apples:
each picked one knocks a dozen to the ground.

Beyond the orchard, through a cloud of fern,
then deep in tiny rustling waves of oak
- a foam of leaf – we paddle down the wood
to find the stream which questionmarks around
old ivy, tattered mushroom, various weed.

You in your wellingtons walk peacefully
into the water, treading trellises
of diamond shapes, a flow of leaded lights,
and herringbone of ripples, brown on brown,
in endless calm repeated corrugations.

And smiling shining up at me you're all
tenderly laced and latticed with the water.
I'm smiling from the bridge, our smilings meet
across the pool, as a precise joy
leaps the approximacy of plain speech.

Then up the sloping wood again, to think
of how it's crammed invisibly with bluebells
buried but going to burst out breathlessly
in Spring, although they're now a mass of brown
hedgehoggy chestnut wrappings in the mud.

'Snowstorm'

(Translation of Pasternak's *Metel'*, 1915)

In this outer quarter where never a foot
stepped except for the foot of a blizzard
or sibyl, steeped in a demon region,
and snows are sleeping a sleep of the dead –

Stop, in this outer quarter where never
foot ever stepped except for a sibyl's
foot or a blizzard's, a wayward shard
of a halter struck at a dormer's glass.

Not a jot to be seen, yet this very quarter
could be a part of a borough, an area
nearer the border (some wanderer, haunter
of midnight, went shying from me with a shudder) –

listen, in this far quarter where never
foot ever stepped, there's no one but murderers.
Lipless and speechless, a spectre, an aspen
leaf is your messenger, whiter than linen.

It knocked at all portals, it hurtled and tossed,
peered round in a spiral of snow from the road . . .
'This is not the right city, it's not the right midnight,
and you, night's herald – you're utterly lost!'

But you whispered a purposeful message to me.

In this outer quarter where biped never . . .

I too am utterly lost . . . I'm a sort of . . .

'Not the right midnight, not the right city.'

‘Winter morning'

(Translation of Pasternak's *Zimnee utro*, 1922)

Air falls in little grey plaits and pleats.
With fugitive glances the snow recalls
'time for bye-byes', the whispers, the treacle,
while day sank behind the cradle.

Go out and you shiver all over, your skin
stings and tingles . . . satchels, children,
the street being folded down in quiet
pleats of grey fishing-net.

All things were folded: the fox in the fable
who flung out fish from a truck,
tree, shed, knitting-needles, mittens,
wintry air, wonderstruck.

Later, by flower-pots, under the bird-cage,
wasn't it arithmetic's pleating and plotting
that chilled the school-desk from out in the open,
blowing and snowing?

Your aching tooth would be treated, anointed,
but the doctor's eye had in it a madness,
ruled and chequered, of school-bags and snowballs,
sums full of sleepy scrawls.

Today the same wintry and purring fable
rustles like snow across my gazette,
thrown past a foam of manes and pavements
like grey fishing-net.

Tiny-windowed, freezing, fleecy,
that same old weirdness of nestless birches
rolls clothy night up at dawn, over tea-cups.
Wintry air, wonderstruck.

Thistle

The wind shifted,

and even the stately six-foot thistle

let its great fangs be lifted.

Notes

P.9:

Line 6 - 'metta': (in Theravada Buddhism) meditation focused on the development of unconditional love for all beings. Pali word for 'loving-kindness'.

P.12:

Terence Doherty: teacher of biology and art at Colchester Royal Grammar School, who died in 1983.

P.17:

Line 2 - Boris Pasternak: "There is no anguish that snow cannot cure".

Line 8 - Josef Brodsky: "I was born and brought up in the Baltic marshland".

P.15:

My friend Valya's body was cremated two years after her death, given back to us by the medical research people.

P.24

I was reading O.B.'s poem about Walberswick (Suffolk) while travelling by train in Russia in 1996; my poem repeats the rhyme and metre patterns of his poem.

P.26:

The bells of St Mary's Church at East Bergholt are hung in a ground-level cage.

P.31:

"In the closeness of people there is a secret boundary ..." Anna Akhmatova.

P.31

"Schlagbaum", a barrier.

P.32:

This poem is based on Pasternak's 'Hamlet', the first of the Doctor Zhivago poems.

P.33:

One of two poems written while reading Geoffrey Hill's 'The Triumph of Love'. The second is on page 34.